MW01703582

On Ma Journey Now

LEADER

Ouida Board Rush Scarborough–
Hodnett
1805 Belcrest Drive
Greensboro, NC 27406

Abingdon Press | Nashville

ON MA JOURNEY NOW:
A LENTEN STUDY BASED ON AFRICAN AMERICAN SPIRITUALS
LEADER GUIDE

Copyright © 2005 by Abingdon Press

All rights reserved.

No part of this work may be reproduced or transmitted in any form or by any means, electronic or mechanical, including photocopying and recording, or by any information storage or retrieval system, except as may be expressly permitted by the 1976 Copyright Act or in writing from the publisher. Requests for permission should be addressed in writing to Permissions Office, 201 Eighth Avenue, South, P.O. Box 801, Nashville, Tennessee 37202-0801 or e-mailed to permissions@abingdonpress.com.

Scripture quotations in this publication, unless otherwise indicated, are from the New Revised Standard Version of the Bible, copyright © 1989 by the Division of Christian Education of the National Council of the Churches of Christ in the United States of America, and are used by permission.

This book is printed on acid-free, elemental chlorine-free paper.

ISBN 0-687-05362-5

Lead Editor: Marilyn E. Thornton

05 06 07 08 09 10 11 12 3 14 —10 9 8 7 6 5 4 3 2 1

MANUFACTURED IN THE UNITED STATES OF AMERICA

Ouida Rush-Hodnett
1805 Belcrest Drive
G'boro, NC
27406

Contents

Introduction

On *Ma Journey Now: A Lenten Study Based on African American Spirituals* is the sixth in a series of Bible studies that utilize both Scripture and song to interpret God's movement in our lives and in the world. The first in the series is *Plenty Good Room* (2002), followed by the Advent study *Mary Had a Baby* (2003), then *Ride On, Jesus* (2004), *Come Out de Wilderness* (spring 2005), and *Don't Let This Harvest Pass* (fall 2005). The entire series uses the African American spiritual as a way of centering the perspective, culture, history, and needs of the African American community in the study of the Bible. *On Ma Journey Now* is designed for study during the Lenten season.

In *On Ma Journey Now,* we cry aloud in song through the African American spiritual. Most of the spirituals used in this study are "sorrow songs," melodies that lament, mourn, and grieve a particular situation. Coming from the souls of African American slaves, these songs are uniquely appropriate for drawing us into a period of mourning for our own sins as well as for the sins of the world. As you prepare, pay special attention to the boxes in each session of the Student Book that contain quotes from those who had been enslaved. Invite your students to moan and mourn with the slaves, to travel with Jesus as he shows us how to resist the evils of the world, and to gather strength for the journey of life.

Preparing to Lead the Study

The Leader Guide is designed to assist you in guiding participants through an enriching learning experience. It contains ideas that can help you with preparation and instruction. With the CD and the Student and Leader Books of the *On Ma Journey Now* Bible study, you have everything you need to lead a group successfully.

The Music

The spirituals for each session are on the accompanying CD. The singer is Diana Poe, a professor and artist-in-residence at Tennessee State University in Nashville. She is accompanied by Reginald Green on the piano. The arrangements are designed to invite participants not only to meditate on the music but also to sing along. Your familiarity with them will help your students take this American folk art form seriously, enjoying the musical qualities as well as the biblical foundations. You will need a CD player for each session. “I Want Jesus to Walk With Me” (# 1) is a bonus track, included purely for purposes of prayer and meditation. There is no session based on this spiritual. Enjoy!

Bible Study

Be familiar with the Bible lesson for each session, and read the indicated Scripture. Each session contains a key verse, opening prayer, the spiritual lyrics, musical description, socio-historical background information, contextual interpretations of the Scripture lessons, “Ponder and Wonder” sections, “Food for Thought” questions, and a closing prayer. The text helps to provoke thought on historical and contemporary issues, providing opportunities for discussion. Thoroughly read each session in the Student Book.

The Group Meeting

Create a setting that helps the learning process. Much can be learned from symbols, colors, and architecture. Prepare a common center table or altar. Cover the table with different textures of cotton and plain burlap (fabrics used within the slave community). Place on the table items such as artifacts, photographs, or other visuals that relate thematically to the study. Encourage group members to contribute.

Be welcoming as participants arrive. Be sure to have the spiritual playing for the session. Begin each session with silent meditation and opening prayer. Give a short review of the main points of the last session, and allow group members to share their insights.

As the session continues, include other notes and questions regarding the material to encourage group discussion and individual contemplation. Encourage students to identify at least one important point they learned and one step each will take to apply that learning. In closing, suggest some ideas for preparing for the next session.

Suggested Steps for Preparing for Each Session

Step 1: Prepare for the study. Get your favorite chair with a pen and pad handy, or type your notes into a computer. Remember the CD player. Listen to track # 1 on the CD, "I Want Jesus to Walk With Me."

Step 2: Take a few minutes of quiet time. Light a candle, meditate, and pray.

Step 3: Read the Scripture and lyrics, and listen to the spiritual for the session.

Step 4: As you listen, write any thoughts or emotional responses you might have. What are your first impressions? What are some cultural, social, or historical images that stand out for you? What other biblical references come to mind?

Step 5: Read and reflect on the session material. Write down your questions and concerns. As you continue your study, utilize other commentary or support literature. Write down your reflections.

Session 1

This Lonesome Valley

Matthew 4:1-4

Key Verse: But he [Jesus] answered, "It is written, 'One does not live by bread alone, / but by every word that comes from the mouth of God'" (Matthew 4:4).

"Jesus Walked This Lonesome Valley"

Chorus:
Jesus walked this lonesome valley.
He had to walk it by himself.
Oh, nobody else could walk it for him.
He had to walk it by himself.

I must walk this lonesome valley.
We must walk this lonesome valley.

Opening

1. Play "Jesus Walked This Lonesome Valley" (# 2 on CD) as the participants enter the room.
2. Welcome group members and lead them in a centering moment. You may want to play "I Want Jesus to Walk With Me" (# 1 on CD) at this time.
3. Prayer (page 7, Student Book): **O God, you are our comfort. You come to us when we are lonely and depressed. Help us see the needs of others and share your comfort with them. Amen.**
4. Conversation Starter: Allow participants to introduce themselves by telling what they hope to learn from this study. Introduce yourself. Have an opening discussion about general impressions of African American spirituals. Play the spiritual (# 2 on CD) again. Ask the group to write down one response/reaction from listening.

Let's Listen: A Song of Freedom; The Middle Passage

1. After listening to the lesson spiritual (# 2 on CD) once more, have participants read these sections aloud. Ask participants to share any stories, personal anecdotes, or testimonies related to the spiritual and the Middle Passage.
2. Ask: **What does "Jesus Walked This Lonesome Valley" tell you about the experience of the slaves during the Middle Passage? How could the slaves survive such a tragedy?**

The Wilderness: Matthew 4:1-3

Ask for a volunteer to read aloud Matthew 4:1-3. Then ask group members to read this section silently. Allow discussion on any questions or insights.

The First Test: Matthew 4:4

1. Read Matthew 4:4. Have group members share their first impressions. Then have this section read.
2. Ask: **What does the first test represent? How does Jesus' test relate to your time(s) of testing?** Give everyone the opportunity to respond.

Ponder and Wonder: Wilderness Experience

1. After having this section read, divide the class into smaller groups. Assign each group a question from "Food for Thought" (page 12, Student Book). Allow five minutes for discussion.
2. As everyone returns to the larger group, ask a representative from each group to share insights from their discussion.

Closing

1. Give a brief synopsis of some main points of the lesson. As you thank everyone for coming, encourage their return by announcing information concerning the next session.
2. Close with prayer (page 12, Student Book): **Gracious God, you have blessed us to live in community, never to be alone. Help us always to recognize that we should help and support each other. Amen.**

Session 2

A City Called Heaven

Matthew 4:5-7

Key Verse: Jesus said to him, "Again it is written, 'Do not put the Lord your God to the test'" (Matthew 4:7).

"A City Called Heaven"

I am a poor pilgrim of sorrow.
I'm tossed in this wide world alone.
No hope have I for the morrow.
I'm tryin' to make heaven my home.
Sometimes I am tossed and driven, Lord.
Sometimes I don't know where to roam.
I've heard of a city called heaven.
I've started to make heaven my home.

Opening

1. Play "A City Called Heaven" (# 3 on CD) as the participants enter the room.
2. Welcome group members and lead them in a centering moment. You may want to play "I Want Jesus to Walk With Me" (# 1 on CD) at this time.
3. Prayer (page 13, Student Book): **Dear God, Creator of heaven and earth, in you we find hope. Teach us to follow you more closely so that we may bring hope to others. Amen.**
4. Conversation Starter: Open the session with a discussion on heaven as a metaphor. Ask: **What constitutes heaven in today's world? Is it money, a nice house, health, wealth, and happiness?**

Let's Listen: A Song of Despair and Hope

1. Play the lesson spiritual (# 3 on CD) again. Invite participants to read aloud this section.
2. Ask group members about their experience with the spiritual.

Pilgrims of Sorrow

Ask for a volunteer to read this section. Discuss any questions or insights that may arise.

Heard of a City

Have the class read this section.

The Second Test: Matthew 4:5-7

1. Briefly review the first test from Session One (page 11, Student Book).
2. Ask a group member to read the Scripture lesson aloud. Then ask participants for their first impressions from hearing the Scripture.
3. Now read this section. Let each member share his or her impressions.
4. Ask: **Why do you think Jesus responded with "it is written" and the Scripture when the devil was testing him? What does this say to you for your times of testing?**

Ponder and Wonder: Resisting Temptation

1. Read this section.
2. Divide the class into smaller groups and assign each group a question from "Food for Thought" (page 18, Student Book). Allow five minutes for discussion.
3. As everyone returns to the larger group, ask a representative from each group to share insights from the discussion.

Closing

1. Review the main points of the lesson.
2. Have the group form a circle, join hands, and close with prayer (page 18, Student Book): **Oh gracious God, our strength in times of weakness, remembering our failures is bitter to us. Help us to depend on you for our help and to help others in their time of temptation. For Christ's sake we pray. Amen.**

Session 3

Bow Down on Your Knees

Matthew 4:8-11

Key Verse: Jesus said to him, "Away with you Satan! for it is written, 'Worship the Lord your God / and serve only him" (Matthew 4:10).

"Po' Mou'ner's Got a Home at Last"

Refrain:
No harm, no harm, go tell Brother Elijah,
No harm, no harm, po' mou'ner's got a home at last.

Verse 1:
Mou'ner, mou'ner, ain't you tired o' mou'nin'?
Bow down on your knees and pray.
Mou'ner, mou'ner, ain't you tired o' mou'nin'?
J'ine (join) de band with the angels.

Verse 2:
Sinner, sinner, ain't you tired o' sinnin'?

Verse 3:
Gambler, gambler, ain't you tired o' gamblin'?

Opening

1. Play "Po' Mou'ner's Got a Home at Last" (# 4 on CD) as the participants enter the room.
2. Welcome group members and lead them in silent meditation. You may want to play "I Want Jesus to Walk With Me" (# 1 on CD) at this time.

3. Prayer (page 19, Student Book): **Dear Jesus, our Redeemer and Lord, in you we find shelter. Help us always to know that we have a home in you, a special place prepared for us.**
4. Conversation Starter: Describe a time in your life—other than an event of death—when you were in mourning.

Let's Listen: Blessing Those Who Mourn

1. Play the lesson spiritual (# 4 on CD) again.
2. Invite participants to read this section silently. Address any questions or insights that may arise.

Po' Mou'ner's Got a Home

1. Have a participant to read this section.
2. Ask: **How can you make a place of peace and comfort in slavery? How did the slaves find a new home, community, and acceptance?** Pause for insights and reflection.

The Last Test: Matthew 4:8-11

1. Review Jesus' responses to the first and second tests (Matthew 4:4, 7).
2. Ask a volunteer to read the Scripture lesson aloud. Then have the first two paragraphs of this section read. Ask the following questions: **What is the point of testing? What is it in your life that Satan uses to test you? How can people of faith withstand and confront temptation?**
3. After discussion, continue reading this section. Ask: **What does it mean to desire the crown without the cross?**

Ponder and Wonder: Worship

1. Briefly discuss each "Food for Thought" question with the entire group (page 24, Student Book).
2. Help students identify at least one point that they have learned and can use in their lives.

Closing

Prayer (page 24, Student Book): **Gracious, dear Jesus, we love you. You are our source of peace. Teach us how to worship you in spirit and truth so that we can always find a home in your presence. Amen.**

Session 4

I Couldn't Hear Nobody Pray

Luke 6:12-16

Key Verse: Now during those days he [Jesus] went out to the mountain to pray; and he spent the night in prayer to God (Luke 6:12).

"I Couldn't Hear Nobody Pray"

O, I couldn't hear nobody pray.
I couldn't hear nobody pray.
O, way down yonder by myself,
And I couldn't hear nobody pray.

In the mornin'.
In the noonday.
In the evenin'.

Opening

1. Before this session, you may want to place on the common table symbols of prayer such as a book of prayers or a picture or statue of praying hands.
2. Play "I Couldn't Hear Nobody Pray" (# 5 on CD) as the participants enter the room.
3. Welcome group members and lead them in a centering moment. You may want to play "I Want Jesus to Walk With Me" (# 1 on CD) at this time.
4. Prayer (page 25, Student Book): **O God, you are our peace. In you we find a solace. Give us the will to keep praying and trusting that you will hear and respond. In Jesus' name. Amen.**

5. Conversation Starter: **How can the lyrics of this lesson's spiritual inform your prayer life?** ("Food for Thought" Question # 1—page 30, Student Book).

Let's Listen: A Song of Community

1. Play the lesson spiritual (# 5 on CD) again. Then read this section.
2. Ask: **What makes this a song of community?** Give some time for discussion.

The Hush Arbor: The Invisible Church

Invite participants to read this section aloud. Ask for comments concerning the opinions of Bishop Daniel Payne.

All Night Prayer Time: Luke 6:12

1. Read the Scripture lesson. Then have this section read.
2. Start a discussion on the meaning of prayer by asking: **Does prayer help you in your daily walk? How often do you pray each day and for how long?**

Choosing Apostles: Luke 6:13-16

1. Read the Scripture lesson. Then ask participants to read this section.
2. If there is time, assign students to look up each Scripture reference and read them aloud.

Ponder and Wonder: Prayer Warriors

1. After having this section read, divide the class into smaller groups and assign the remaining "Food for Thought" questions (page 30, Student Book).
2. As everyone returns to the big group, have them share the main points of their discussion.

Closing

1. Briefly summarize the lesson.
2. Play the spiritual again softly as you close with prayer: **Dear Lord, give me a praying spirit. Help me truly to mean the prayer that you taught the disciples:** (pray the Lord's Prayer—page 30, Student Book).

Session 5

On Ma Journey Now, Mt. Zine (Zion)

Mark 10:32-34

Key Verse: See, we are going up to Jerusalem, and the Son of Man will be handed over to the chief priests and the scribes, and they will condemn him to death; then they will hand him over to the Gentiles (Mark 10:33).

"On Ma Journey Now, Mt. Zine (Zion)"

Chorus:
On ma journey now, Mt. Zine,
On ma journey now, Mt. Zine.
Well, I wouldn't take nothin', Mt. Zine,
For ma journey now, Mt. Zine.

Verse 1:
One day, one day, I was walking along.
Well, the elements opened and the love came down.

Verse 2:
I went to the valley but I didn't go to stay.
Ma soul got happy an' I stayed all day.

Verse 3:
Just talk about me just as much as you please.
Well, I'll talk about you when I bend ma knees.

Opening

1. Play "On Ma Journey Now, Mt. Zine" (# 6 on CD) as the participants enter the room.

2. Welcome group members and lead them in a short silent meditation. You may want to play "I Want Jesus to Walk With Me" (# 1 on CD) at this time.
3. Prayer (page 31, Student Book): **Lord God, in you we find strength to move forward. Give us the courage and determination to continue the journey. In Jesus' name. Amen.**
4. Conversation Starters: Choose one and have a brief discussion.
   a. What does it mean to be on a Christian journey?
   b. How do you handle negative/destructive criticism?
   c. What is the evidence of spiritual growth in your life?

Let's Listen: A Song of Courage and Determination

1. Play the lesson spiritual (# 6 on CD) again and have this section read.
2. Have students recall a time in which courage and determination were necessary in their lives.

Mark 10:32-34: On the Way to Jerusalem

1. Have the Scripture lesson read. Play "On Ma Journey Now" again. Encourage participants to fill in with the piano, singing "Mt. Zion."
2. Read this section.

Persecution

1. Select a participant to read this section. Discuss.
2. Pay particular attention to the endnote regarding *Clotel* on page 45 of the Student Book.

Ponder and Wonder: Suffering Servant

After reading this section, have the group discuss the "Food for Thought" questions (pages 35–36, Student Book).

Closing

Close with prayer (page 36, Student Book): **O God, you are our ever-present help in time of trouble. Give us the desire and ability to help others through their struggles. In Jesus' name. Amen.**

Session 6

Were You There?

Mark 15:25-33, 37-39, 46-47

Key Verse: Truly this man was God's Son! (Mark 15:39b).

"Were You There?"

Verse 1:
Were you there when they crucified my Lord?
Were you there when they crucified my Lord?
Oh! sometimes it causes me to tremble, tremble, tremble.
Were you there when they crucified my Lord?

Verse 2:
Were you there when they nailed him to the tree?
Were you there when they nailed him to the tree?
Oh! sometimes it causes me to tremble, tremble, tremble.
Were you there when they nailed him to the tree?

Verse 3:
Were you there when the sun refused to shine?
Were you there when the sun refused to shine?
Oh! sometimes it causes me to tremble, tremble, tremble.
Were you there when the sun refused to shine?

Opening

1. Play "Were You There?" (# 7 on CD) as the participants enter the room.
2. Welcome group members and lead them in a moment of centering.
3. Prayer (page 37, Student Book): **Holy God, when we cry out, grant us the grace of your hearing, your presence, and your hope. For Christ's sake. Amen.**

4. Conversation Starter: Allow participants to express one thing that has impacted them as a result of participating in this Bible study.

Let's Listen: A Song of Accountability

1. Play "Were You There?" (# 7 on CD) again. Ask participants to listen silently and meditate.
2. Invite group members to read this section. Allow each participant to share impressions about the spiritual. Discuss any questions or insights that may arise.

Who Is "They"?

1. Have this section read aloud. Offer any insights or additional information you may have concerning the nature of betrayal.
2. Discuss "Food for Thought" Question # 2 (page 43, Student Book): **How do we know that we are part of the "they" who crucified Jesus?**

Mark 15:25-33, 37-39: The Crucifixion

Have the Scripture lesson read. Then read this section.

Mark 15:46-47: The Burial of Jesus

Read the Scripture and this section.

The Tree

1. Ask a volunteer to read this section aloud.
2. You may have access to a recording of "Strange Fruit." If so and if there is time, play it for the class. Singer India.Arie does a rendition of this song in a documentary concert about the blues entitled *Lightning in a Bottle*. It is available at Blockbuster movie rentals, and the soundtrack is available on CD.
3. **Ida B. Wells Barnett (1862–1931)**

   A great political reformer, Wells Barnett was born a slave in Holly Springs, Mississippi, six months before the Emancipation Proclamation. In 1889, she was elected secretary of the Colored Press Association. She created her own newspaper, *Free Speech and Headlight*; was cofounder of the NAACP; and founded the Negro

Fellowship League, a social center with reading rooms and a dormitory for black men. She also agitated for African American women's right to vote.[1]

Ponder and Wonder: Repentance

After reading this section, choose several "Food for Thought" questions for discussion (page 43, Student Book).

Closing

1. After your closing remarks, have a prayer (page 43, Student Book): **Dear God, thank you for your grace and mercy. Empower us to be gracious and merciful to others. Thank you for showing us such love. Enable us to be channels of the love of Jesus Christ in this world. In Jesus' name we pray. Amen.**
2. As everyone is preparing to leave, continue playing the spirituals.

---

[1] See *The African American Century: How Black Americans Have Shaped Our Country,* by Henry Louis Gates Jr. and Cornel West (The Free Press, 2000); pages 35–38.